David and Goliath

Ruth F. Brin

illustrated by H. Hechtkopf

Lerner Publications Company
Minneapolis

for Noah Gabriel Ingber

AN OUTSTANDING SELECTION FROM *Israel*

OLD TESTAMENT STORIES
Illustrated by H. Hechtkopf

Jonah's Journey

The Story of Esther

A Basket in the Reeds
The Story of Moses

Mission on a Mountain
The Story of Abraham and Isaac

David and Goliath

First published in the United States of America 1977
by Lerner Publications Company, Minneapolis, Minnesota
All English language rights reserved.

Text copyright © 1977 by Lerner Publications Company, Minneapolis
Illustrations copyright © 1977 by Massada Press Ltd., Ramat-Gan, Israel

International Standard Book Number: 0-8225-0365-4
Library of Congress Catalog Card Number: 76-23741

Manufactured in the United States of America

2 3 4 5 6 7 8 9 10 85 84 83 82 81 80

Long ago, in the ancient days of Israel, a young boy named David lived with his family on a farm near Bethlehem. In the fields nearby, the family grew wheat and barley. Farther away, among the rocky hills, were green pastures where they kept a flock of sheep.

David was the youngest of eight brothers. Six of the brothers worked with their father, Jesse, in the fields. The seventh brother, Shammah, was the shepherd for the family's sheep. When David was seven years old, Shammah began to teach him how to take care of the flock.

Shammah told David that during the winter, when it rained often, there was plenty of grass in the nearby pastures for the sheep to eat. But in the hot, dry summer, Shammah had to take the sheep far from home to find food. Then he spent his nights and days alone in the wilderness.

Shammah taught David how to find his way in the wilderness, and where to get water during the dry summer months. He also made David a sling—a weapon shepherds needed to protect their sheep from wild animals. David learned how to choose a round, smooth stone to fit his sling. Shammah showed him how to twirl the sling so that the stone flew far into the air. At first, the stone went off in all directions, but Shammah patiently taught David how to aim it.

After a while, David found that if he ran forward while circling his sling, his aim was better. But when he came home to show off his new trick to his oldest brother, Eliab, he missed his target. Eliab laughed at him.

"Now will you sing a song about what a great slinger you are, little one?" he teased.

Poor David! Everyone knew he liked to make up songs, but Eliab never tired of teasing him about it.

As time passed, David grew to love music more and more, despite Eliab's teasing. He was becoming a fine singer, as well as a good shepherd. But he longed to have an instrument of his own, so he could accompany himself as he made up new songs.

When David was thirteen, his father gave him a lyre, a small stringed instrument something like a harp. David was delighted, for he could carry the lyre with him when he went into the pastures. Now that he was old enough, he sometimes took care of the sheep by himself. He often sang and played while he watched over them. On bright spring days, when red poppies bloomed on the hillsides, David sang a song of thanks to God for His beautiful world:

> I live in a delightful country,
> Lovely indeed is my place. . . .
> I bless the Lord who guided me.
> He is at my right hand; I am never afraid.
>
> *Psalms 16:6, 8*

In the calm evenings, David looked up at the stars and felt that God was very close to him. "The heavens declare the glory of God," he sang, "and the sky shows us His handiwork." *(Psalms 19:2)*

David spent many happy days in the pastures that spring. But his life did not remain so peaceful. Not far from the quiet hills and pastures, the armies of Israel were preparing for war with their powerful enemies the Philistines. One evening, when David returned home from the pasture, he found that three of his brothers were gone. Shammah, Abinadab, and Eliab had joined the army of Saul, king of Israel.

Jesse called David to his side. "Well, my son," he said, "there will be twice as much work for us to do, now that three of your brothers are gone. Since you've taken such good care of the sheep in these past few months, I want you to take Shammah's place as the shepherd. From now on, you'll be the only one responsible for the flock."

"Don't worry," David answered. "I can manage."

Yes," his father said, ruffling David's sandy hair, "of course you will manage. But remember, there are lions in the hills. Now that the dry months are coming, wild game is scarce. The lions sometimes get hungry for sheep."

David promised to be careful. He felt afraid, but he tried not to show his fear.

Early the next morning, David took his sheep and went far into the wilderness in search of good pasture. That night he could find no shelter for the flock. So he gathered some brush and loose rocks and made a rough pen. Then he lay down on his sheepskin blanket to sleep.

During the night the flock began to stir. David woke with a start. There was a bright moon, and the sheep were awake, crowding silently together at one end of the pen.

Then David saw a movement in the shadows. His sling was tied to his wrist, as always, and he reached into his bag for a smooth, round stone. The shadow moved again—it was a big animal, maybe a lion. If his first shot injured the animal but didn't kill it, it might attack him! He had a knife in his belt, but it was useless until the animal came closer.

The creature began to move slowly out of the shadows, flowing like water over the rough fence David had built. As it raised its head, David saw the gleam of its eyes. He twirled his sling and let fly.

The animal leaped into the air with a great roar and fell to the ground. David waited. The creature shuddered, then lay still. Clutching his knife, David crept toward it slowly. The animal was probably stunned, not really dead. Now he saw that it was a lion—a huge male with a full mane.

David quickly plunged his knife into its neck and then backed away. But no paw was lifted. The lion was truly dead.

David took a deep breath. He felt shaky. "What if the lion had seen me or leaped at me?" he thought. "Surely, God was with me."

He dragged the body away from the pen and returned to count his sheep. They were afraid, too—bleating loudly and moving about in the pen. To calm them, David took up his lyre and began to pluck a few notes. He thought of his brothers, and of how the Philistines might be hunting them down, the way the lion hunted the sheep. He began to sing:

> O Lord, My God, in You I seek refuge.
> Deliver me from all my pursuers and save me,
> Lest, like a lion, they tear me in pieces . . . .
> *Psalms 7:2-3*

After he had sung awhile, David finally slept.

The next morning, he decided to return to the farm and tell his father about the lion. He cut off the brush from the lion's tail to take home. When he left, the vultures were already at the carcass. Soon they would pick it clean.

When David reached home, his father had news for him. "We have received a message from your brothers," Jesse said. "They are camping in the Valley of the Acacias, and they want us to send food. The Philistine armies are drawn up on one side of the valley, and our army is on the other. Every day a huge giant comes out from among the Philistines, dressed in heavy armor, and challenges the men of Israel to fight."

"And who has fought him?" asked David.

"No one," said his father. "They say he is nine feet tall."

"Cowards!" cried David. "I don't believe there is any man that tall!"

"It's easy for you to talk bravely," said his father, "you're just a boy . . . ."

David suddenly remembered his adventure. "Maybe I'm just a boy," he said, "but look here, Father!" And he brought out the lion's brush. "I killed a lion—and he never had a chance to kill any of your sheep!"

Jesse's face went white. "You killed a lion, my son, all alone, out in the wilderness! God be thanked for your safety."

David nodded his head. Suddenly he didn't feel so bold after all.

"Well," said Jesse, "now that the lions are beginning to prowl, I had better hire two men from the village and send them out with the sheep. I don't want you to take such a chance again. Besides, someone must carry food to your brothers. You can take some parched grain—that's a treat for your brothers—and ten loaves of bread, and also ten cheeses for King Saul, as a gift from me. You can make the trip easily in a day with a donkey to carry the food. Give your brothers my greetings and bring back news from them." He patted David's shoulder, and added thoughtfully, "They tell me the king has offered a great reward to any man who will kill this giant, Goliath."

"Why doesn't the king kill Goliath?" asked David. "I thought Saul was a great warrior."

"Indeed he is. But they say he has somehow displeased God. Lately he gets into terrible moods—sometimes he is angry and other times very sad. Even his son, Jonathan, can't comfort him. Jonathan is about your age, you know."

But David hardly heard these words. He was already thinking of his coming adventure. "Father," he said, "I will gather the things together and leave this morning."

"Peace and blessings to you, my son," said Jesse. "And I'm proud that you killed that lion."

"Peace to you too, Father. I'll be back in three days' time, or sooner." David did not know that it would be a good while longer before he saw his father again.

David's journey was hot but not difficult, and he arrived at the soldiers' camp just before sundown. He wandered aimlessly amidst the smoke of cooking fires and the groups of soldiers who hurried about, preparing for the next day's battle. At last he found his brothers.

They were glad to see him and invited him to sit by their fire and share their evening meal. That night he lay in their tent and fell asleep wondering what it would be like to be a grown man and a soldier.

At dawn, David awoke to the sound of trumpets. He dressed quickly and rushed to the battle line with his brothers. Across the valley stood the Philistine soldiers, armed with spears, bows, and arrows. Then, out stepped Goliath. Truly, he was the tallest man David had ever seen. He swaggered up and down between the front lines of the two armies. David saw the sun flash on his bronze helmet and coat of mail. He had bronze armor on his legs and a bronze javelin slung across his shoulders. In his hand was a huge spear with a heavy iron head. His shield bearer marched before him, dwarfed by Goliath.

Then the giant shouted to the soldiers of Israel, "Why do all of you come out to the battle line? Am I not a Philistine and are you not all soldiers of Saul? Let one man come forward from each side to decide this battle! Choose a man for yourselves and let him come to me. If he kills me, the Philistines shall serve you. But if I kill him, you shall be our slaves. I defy Israel this day!" And he roared with a mighty voice and shook his spear in the air. "Give me a man that I may fight!"

He waited for a moment, staring fiercely at the Israelites. But Saul and his army were afraid and did nothing. So Goliath turned and strode back to the Philistine camp, his armor clanking with every step.

After the giant was gone, David said to Eliab, "Who is this Philistine, that he should defy the armies of God? Why doesn't someone kill him and stop his boasting?"

Eliab always teased David, but this time he was really angry. "You want to see someone killed!" he shouted. "Me, I suppose. You left your sheep and you, a little boy, come to tell us what to do. You want to see a battle, but you don't know what war is!"

David answered, "What have I done now? I only asked a question . . ." Then he turned to Shammah and asked, "If this is the army of God, why are the men afraid?" And Shammah tried to quiet him, asking if he had seen the armor and the huge size of the man.

Some soldiers overheard David's conversation with his brothers, and they told King Saul what he had said. Saul sent word for David to come to his tent. By the time David reached the great tent of the king, he understood that no soldier of Israel dared to fight the giant.

David said to Saul, "I am your servant, and I am not afraid to go and fight Goliath."

Saul looked curiously at the slight young man with the sandy hair. But he didn't laugh. He said, "You are only a youth, and untrained in the arts of war."

David answered, "At home, when I watched my father's sheep, I had to kill a fierce lion. Surely this Philistine who defies God's army is no better than a lion. The Lord delivered me from the lion's jaws, and I believe He will also save me from the hands of the Philistine."

Saul saw that David was determined, so he said, "You must take my armor then, if you are going out to fight him."

The armor bearers brought Saul's bronze helmet, his coat of mail, and his great sword. But when David put them on, he could hardly walk. Everything was much too heavy and too big for him. He was glad his brother Eliab wasn't there to laugh at him.

He struggled out of the armor, saying he wasn't used to it. "I must fight the giant with my own weapons," he told the king.

The next morning, David stopped at the brook and carefully chose five smooth stones. He put them in his shepherd's bag. Then he tied his sling to his right wrist and took up his shepherd's staff.

When Goliath came to shout at the men of Israel, David stepped forward from the line. As David faced him, carrying his staff, Goliath snarled, "Am I a dog, that you come to me with a stick?" And he cursed David to his Philistine gods. "Come to me, little one, and I will give your flesh to the vultures!"

David remembered the dead lion and shuddered, but he answered bravely, "You come to me with sword and spear, but I come to you in the name of the Lord, the God of the armies of Israel, whom you have defied. This day the Lord will deliver you to me!"

His voice rang out clear and strong, but David felt very much afraid. Behind him, he heard the Israelites murmuring fearfully among themselves. "How could such a small boy fight the giant?" they were saying. "Surely he will be torn to pieces!"

But David knew what he must do. With trembling fingers, he fitted a stone into his sling. Suddenly he ran forward, circling his arm rapidly in the air. Goliath raised his spear, but before he could throw it, David's stone struck him in the forehead.

Goliath's spear slipped from his hand, and he fell face-down on the ground with a terrible crash. David ran and stood over the Philistine. He pulled Goliath's huge, heavy sword from its sheath and brought the blade down on the giant with all his strength.

After the Philistines saw that David had killed their
champion, they turned and began to run. The men of
Israel rushed forward with a great shout and chased
their enemies over the hills.

When David returned to Saul's tent, Saul was amazed to hear what he had done. The king was very grateful, and he asked David to come and live with him. Jonathan, Saul's son, gave David his princely robe to wear, and his armor and his sword. From that time on, David and Jonathan were very close friends.

David remained with Saul and Jonathan for a long time. Whenever Saul was sad, David would play his lyre and sing to him. And the song Saul loved most was one that David sang to remember his days in the wilderness with his father's sheep:

> The Lord is my shepherd,
> I shall not want.
> He makes me lie down in green pastures,
> He leads me beside quiet waters,
> He restores my soul.
> He guides me in right paths for His Name's sake.
> Even though I walk through the valley of the shadow of death,
> I shall not fear, for You are with me . . . .

Psalms 23:1-4